Keep Your
Coooooool!

Stress Reducing Strategies for Key Stage 2 and 3

George Robinson
and
Tina Rae

Illustrated by Tina Rae

Lucky Duck is more than a publishing house and training agency. George Robinson and Barbara Maines founded the company in the 1980s when they worked together as a head and psychologist developing innovative strategies to support challenging students.

They have an international reputation for their work on bullying, self-esteem, emotional literacy and many other subjects of interest to the world of education.

George and Barbara have set up a regular news-spot on the website. Twice yearly these items will be printed as a newsletter. If you would like to go on the mailing list to receive this then please contact us:

Lucky Duck Publishing Ltd. 3 Thorndale Mews, Clifton, Bristol, BS8 2HX, UK

Phone: 44 (0)117 973 2881   e-mail newsletter@luckyduck.co.uk
Fax: 44 (0)117 973 1707   website www.luckyduck.co.uk

ISBN 1 873 942 93 1

Published by Lucky Duck Publishing Ltd
3 Thorndale Mews, Clifton, Bristol
BS8 2HX, UK

www.luckyduck.co.uk

Page Design Wendy Ogden

Cover Design Helen Weller
Printed by Antony Rowe limited

© George Robinson and Tina Rae 2001

Reprinted April 2002, new format January 2004

Contents

Introduction and Background

Experiencing tension and stress is a normal part of everyday life and, to a certain extent, a necessary one, if individuals are to effectively grow and effect change. What is essential is that such stress is managed effectively and kept to a manageable level so that individuals can maintain 'a healthy balance of tension, growth, rest and self-nurturing' (Rae, T. 2001).

The world is a highly pressurised and rapidly changing place, which clearly influences the mental, physical and emotional health of all those who live within it – both adults and children. Stress is not the singular property of adults. It now unfortunately affects children from all social backgrounds and contexts. Stress-related illnesses are no longer confined to 'grown-ups', but now appear to be affecting young people and children at an increasingly high rate. We have an idolised image of childhood as being the best days of our life. However, we must accept that children, as much as other members of society, face a variety of stressors, and we see how primary aged pupils respond, for example by:

- Changes in behaviour, e.g. being aggressive/withdrawn.
- Being tearful
- Eating disorders
- School attendance problems
- Attention needing
- Drop in performance
- Lying
- Bragging.

It is vital that we, as adults, acknowledge this fact and really begin to cease minimising the stressors that younger people have to cope with. It is no longer helpful to play down the stress caused by a test, a broken friendship, a bully or a teacher who doesn't appear to like you. In the child's mind, experience and emotions, these are the equivalent of the stress caused to an adult by an exam, a broken relationship, a bully, or a boss who doesn't appear to like you. Of course stress is person specific and each individual will be affected differently by different stressors. Some people may relish the thought of an exam, whilst others will be physically sick at the mere thought of a small test. However, what is essential is that all our stressors are acknowledged and not deemed to be 'little' problems by others who may not share a similar difficulty. Minimising other's problems is not helpful – acknowledging them and helping to develop the appropriate coping strategies certainly is.

As well as the obvious stressors that occur in school, children may face stressors outside school, such as:

- Family financial problems
- Family disharmony, especially between parents
- Family break up

- Single parents
- Bereavements
- Abuse - physical, emotional and sexual
- New partners for their parents
- Moving home
- Moving school
- Friends moving away.

We are not suggesting that all children will face all these stressors, we just acknowledge that children have to cope with stress. More than 30% of all marriages in the UK break up. Just look around your class, how many children do not live with both their natural parents?

This book consequently aims to help young people develop the skills that they need in order to maintain good emotional, physical and mental health. The focus is upon helping children to understand stress, how it manifests itself (in themselves and those around them) and to develop a set of skills and coping strategies so that they can both reduce and eliminate stress. It is vital that they feel they can acknowledge that stress is a part of their lives, and of those around them, whilst also gaining the power to cope effectively and feel that they are in control of their lives. Central to this is the importance of communicating their experiences, feelings and problems to others.

How to use the CD-ROM

The CD-ROM contains a PDF file labelled 'Worksheets.pdf' that contains worksheets for each lesson in this resource. You will need Acrobat Reader version 3 or higher to view and print these resources.

The document is set up to print to A4 but you can enlarge the pages to A3 by increasing the output percentage at the point of printing using the page set-up settings for your printer.

Alternatively, you can photocopy the worksheets directly from this book.

Emotional Literacy

There has been a wealth of recent research that highlights how emotionally literate children, having been given opportunities to communicate their experiences, feelings and problems to others, tend to be more confident, assertive and healthy individuals (Apter 1997, Baker 1998). The fact that their mental and physical health is entwined is also highlighted (Goleman 1996, Grant 1992, Rudd 1998 and Baker 1998). It is consequently vital that adults acknowledge children's emotions and nurture their emotional literacy on a continual basis. Teaching life skills such as problem solving, friendship skills, empathy, reflection, valuing oneself, and coping with changes and stressors need to be a part of the curriculum and regarded as equivalent in importance to teaching reading and writing. Indeed, without the former, progress in the latter will generally be impaired.

A crucial aspect of emotional literacy is the ability to cope effectively with emotions. Children need to be skilled in identifying, labelling and coping with their feelings, alongside recognising and appropriately responding to those of others. Gaining such skills will clearly advantage children both in their present and future lives. Schilling (1996) details how such children are more successful in their careers in comparison to those who are less emotionally literate. A central advantage is also the fact that these children are happier both in themselves and within their relationships with others. They achieve more personal and public success in all areas. Surely this is the right of every child and surely it is our duty to attempt to make this a reality?

However, much of the work available for primary pupils is about enhancing self-esteem. We support this type of material. There is a growing awareness of the importance of 'inclusion' and teachers are addressing the issue of ensuring inclusive practice and systems within their institutions. These should naturally include work that addresses children's emotional needs, skills and development. We think one of the areas that is often neglected is how children will acquire these skills. If a child struggles to learn maths, we teach so that they learn. We apply the same principle to emotional development. A key part of any programme will need to focus upon the development of problem solving skills and specifically the skills of self management and stress management. If our children are to be healthy, well adjusted and happy, then they need both the appropriate context and skills to be provided.

The following lessons provide an appropriate context through story. Story provides a safer way to explore sensitive issues. The discussion, worksheets and strategies help the children to learn the necessary skills.

Objectives

The five sessions in this programme have been designed to meet the following objectives:

- To increase self-esteem/self-concept
- To increase emotional literacy
- To enable children to understand how positive thinking and a positive attitude towards change can minimise stress
- To understand the nature and causes of stress in both general and personal terms
- To increase co-operation and empathy amongst the peer group
- To recognise reactions and behaviours that increase stress
- To recognise reactions and behaviours that minimise stress
- To understand and recognise the consequences of a range of stressors in both themselves and others
- To be able to problem solve with peers and use stepped approaches for coping effectively with stress
- To identify and develop a range of personal strategies in order to manage personal stressors
- To understand the importance of emotional support from significant others (friends/ family/teachers etc.) in coping effectively with stress
- To understand how a healthy lifestyle that includes exercise can minimise stress, and how an unhealthy lifestyle can increase stress levels
- To understand how stress can adversely affect muscles and breathing and how making use of progressive relaxation and visualisation techniques can reduce these symptoms
- To encourage children to develop skills of reflection
- To enable children to set realistic and achievable personal targets in terms of managing stress
- To improve children's ability to identify, manage and cope effectively with stress and to consequently reduce levels of stress and anxiety
- To encourage teachers to understand further the stresses faced by children and to adopt and develop the skills that they need within a supportive framework.

The extent to which these objectives are met will indicate the success of the programme.

The Structure of the Programme

Session 1 – What is stress?

The concept of stress is introduced to the children with a story entitled, ' A Testing Time for Arthur'. This describes how Arthur feels prior to his SATs test and how he is eventually able to calm himself by using a deep breathing exercise. Children are asked to consider the nature of stress and who it affects and to distinguish between 'quiet' and 'noisy' responses to stress. They are given the opportunity to practise Arthur's deep breathing strategy and to identify times when they might use this strategy.

Session 2 – Who gets affected by stress?

The story 'Problem Parents for Paula' highlights how adults are affected by stress and how personal stressors can also impact upon those around us. Children are encouraged to consider how parents, friends, teachers and siblings are affected by stress and to try and identify the main causes of stress. The activity highlights how people can respond to stress in a variety of ways e.g. crying, being aggressive, withdrawing and becoming noisy, and asks the children to work out the 'best ' way to respond to such behaviours. There is a focus upon exercise as a stress management tool.

Session 3 – The stresses faced by young people

The story 'Barney's Bullies' highlights some of the stressors that most young children will experience at school: bullying, a change of teacher/school, peer pressure and the stresses attached to being 'different' in some way. Children are introduced to the physiological aspects of stress and encouraged to distinguish between times when stress may be useful to them and when it may be of little or no use. Positive and negative reactions to stress are reinforced and the use of 'calming' music is introduced as a tool for managing some stresses.

Session 4 – Good ways to react to stress

'Worries for Wilma' shows how burying your head in the sand or covering up a problem very often leads to increased stress levels. Children are introduced to the idea that there are some stressors that we may have to learn to manage as we cannot 'magic' them away. Positive strategies and reactions to stress are reinforced and children are encouraged to seek the support of friends to problem solve and manage stress more effectively.

Session 5 – New ways of coping with stress

'Fred's Friends' touches on stresses that result from change, and specifically changes in friendships/friendship groups that all children will encounter, both in and out of school. The session emphasises the importance of acknowledging how strong such reactions to change can be and how a 'Stop, Think and Plan' strategy can help to alleviate some of the stress and help children achieve a more positive outcome for themselves. Children learn to use a Relaxation Script and Visualisation Strategy in order to cope with stress and are encouraged to review the strategies that they have learnt and practised to date.

The Structure of the Sessions

1. Story

The story clearly needs to be read with conviction by the teacher and this should cause no real problem to the majority of Infant and Junior teachers who are highly skilled in this area. The stories are designed to encourage the pupils to identify with the characters and to gain a deeper understanding of how stress affects both themselves and others. The use of story allows sensitive issues to be covered within a safe context i.e. the children do not have to identify their own stressors in a public way, but can initially identify with the character's stressors/stressful situations. The stories also illustrate both negative and positive responses to stress, alongside introducing some specific stress management strategies.

Though we recommend that the teacher reads the story, the stories are presented so that they can be photocopied. You might find it useful to give the pupils a copy of the story after the lesson. These could be kept in a file with the worksheets. The pupils can design a front cover, the stories and worksheets could be supplemented with a reflective activity, i.e. what I have learned.

2. Discussion Time

This section provides the teacher with pointers as to the content of the discussion and presents a series of key questions for the children to consider. Teachers may wish to make use of a Circle Time approach for this part of the lesson when appropriate. However, given the content of these sessions and the fact that no one should be made to feel stressed in having to make a contribution, it may be necessary to set up a series of ground rules for Discussion Time. These might include making use of appropriate listening skills, showing respect for other's views, trying to build on other's ideas and choosing to pass/not make a contribution should they feel unable to do so. The teacher will clearly need to be sensitive towards each individual's needs.

3. Worksheet

The worksheet activity provides children with an opportunity to record their ideas independently as a pair or as one of a small group. There is no hard and fast rule here and this can be left to the teacher's discretion. The majority of worksheets require minimal recording and children who find writing difficult, or who are at the emergent writing stage, can record their ideas in pictures or have a friend or the teacher act as a scribe. What is important is that the children are encouraged to discuss their ideas and responses and are given some time to feedback as and when appropriate.

4   Stress Stopper

A stress management strategy is introduced in each session in the form of a 'Stress Stopper'. It is vital that the children are given the opportunity to practise the strategy in the session. There is no point in just talking through it! If the strategy is to listen to calm music, use a relaxation script or run on the spot, then the children need to do it there and then. Also, it is important to encourage the children to actually use the strategy in their everyday lives. It may be helpful to set specific targets relating to the 'Stress Stopper', e.g. my Stress Stopper target this week is to take a deep breath and count to 20 while I let my breath out slowly, when I see a sum I think I can't do.

The 'Stress Stoppers' introduced in this course are as follows:

- Deep breathing and counting to 20 while slowly releasing the breath
- Taking exercise in order to reduce tension and stress e.g. running on the spot, skipping on the spot and 'shaking down' from head to toes
- Listening to calming music and visualising positives
- Talking through a problem with others who can help
- Using a stepped approach i.e. Traffic Light Method to find solutions to stress related problems
- Visualisation strategies – finding, describing and visualising a 'Peaceful Place'
- Using a Relaxation Script to reduce stress levels.

Children will have opportunities to practise and use all of these strategies whilst also being encouraged to identify, develop and share their own personal stress management skills and ideas.

Follow up Work

Each session includes a list of follow up activities that are generally intended to reinforce and further extend the concepts introduced in the session. These include discussion, poster design, surveys, story writing, collage, investigative work and book making etc. It is not anticipated that the children will be able to complete all these tasks due to time and curriculum constraints. The teacher and the children may wish to select one or two activities as and when appropriate.

A Final Point

As stated in the introduction, stress is a normal part of everyday life for both children and adults. It is consequently vital that individuals can and do develop the skills needed in order to cope effectively and maintain an emotionally and physically healthy lifestyle. This series of lessons aims to provide children with a bank of basic resources and strategies, whilst encouraging them to maintain and further develop a level of emotional literacy that will allow them to effectively cope with change, stress and personal relationships in their everyday lives. However, it is important to point out that these skills and strategies are generally of use with stress that can be 'managed'. Where adults/children have suffered severe trauma, loss or abuse, these skills may well be insufficient in terms of providing support, and specialist therapeutic intervention will be necessary. Clearly, this is not what this resource is about. The main aim here is to provide all children with a basic understanding and set of skills which will enable them to manage everyday stresses in their everyday lives.

When you have completed the five lessons you may want to further develop the work undertaken. Various suggestions are provided in the 'Developing the Programme' page 57.

References

Apter, T. (1997) *The Confident Child*, New York, London: Norton.

Baker, P. (1998) *Here's Health* magazine, March 20-22.

Ballard, J. (1982) *Circlebook,* New York: Irvington.

Bliss, T., Robinson, G. & Maines, B. (1995) *Developing Circle Time*, Bristol: Lucky Duck Publishing Ltd.

Butler, G. & Hope, T. (1995) *Manage Your Mind*: Oxford University Press.

Dore, H. (1990) *Coping with Stress, Help Yourself Guide*: Hamlyn.

Goleman, D. (1996) *Emotional Intelligence*, London: Bloomsbury.

Grant, W.T. (1992) Consortium on the School-Based Promotion of Social Competence, Drug and Alcohol Prevention Curricula, San Francisco: Josey-Bass.

Gross, J. (2000) *The Emotional Literacy Hour*, Bristol: Lucky Duck Publishing Ltd.

Jacobson, E. (1983) *Progressive Relaxation* (2nd Edition), Chicago: University of Chicago Press.

March, J. S. (Ed) (1995) *Anxiety Disorders in Children and Adolescents*, New York: Guildford Press.

Markham, U. (1990) *Helping Children Cope with Stress:* Sheldon Press.

McConnon, S. & McConnon, M. (1992) *Stress – A Personal Skills Course for Young People:* Thomas Nelson.

Miles, S.H. (1992) *Helping Pupils to Cope with Stress*, Lancaster: Framework Press.

Moser, A. (1988) *Don't Pop your Cork on Mondays! The Children's Anti-Stress Book*, Missouri: Landmark Editions.

Murgatroyd, S. & Woolfe, R. (1982) *Coping with Crisis – Understanding and Helping People in Need*: Open University Press.

Rae, T. (2000) *Confidence, Assertiveness and Self-Esteem*, Bristol: Lucky Duck Publishing Ltd.

Rae, T. (2001) *Strictly Stress – A Stress Management Programme for High School Students*, Bristol: Lucky Duck Publishing Ltd.

Rudd, B. (1998) *Talking is for Kids – Emotional Literacy for Infant School Children*, Bristol: Lucky Duck Publishing Ltd.

Schilling, D. (1996) *Emotional Intelligence Level 1*, Torronto. California, Innerchoice Publishing.

White, M.C. (1999) Picture This, Bristol: Lucky Duck Publishing Ltd.

Session 1

What is stress?

A Testing Time for Arthur

Arthur woke up very early in the morning. He knew that it was early because even though he could hear the birds singing, the sky still looked misty and grey. It wasn't really light. He could hear a dog barking down at Number 28.

"I wish I was that dog", he thought to himself. "At least I wouldn't have to go to school and I could have a nice time running around the streets and playing with my friends!"

Arthur crept carefully out of bed so that he didn't wake up his Mum and his younger brother Joseph. He tiptoed down the stairs and into the living room. He didn't go and get any breakfast from the kitchen. He just didn't feel hungry. He actually felt sick – right in the pit of his stomach. It was a horrible feeling like he'd been sick and was waiting for it to happen again – only he hadn't been sick at all, he just felt sick.

"I'll just get a glass of water", he thought and crept back through to the kitchen. Mimi the cat had just made her way in through the cat flap, so Arthur put out a saucer of water for her too.

"Hello Mimi", he said. "I bet you've had a great time out there, I wish I was you. Do you want to swap and be me for today? Then you could go and do the Maths SATs and I could go and play with Basil next door and sit and sun myself on the roof of the shed...it would be great". Arthur bit his lip. He could feel the tears welling up in his eyes.

"I'm not going to cry", he thought, "I'm not – why should I get so wound up over a test?"

Just then he heard his Mum coming down the stairs.

"Hello Arthur", she said, giving him a big hug. "Are you okay? I know it's the test you don't like today, but at least it'll be over soon."

"I know", said Arthur. "It's just like going to the dentist – once you're in there, it's nearly over and it's only a few moments in your life", he said, repeating all the things his Mum had said the day before.

She smiled at him. "I'll get you some breakfast", she said.

After struggling to eat his cereal, Arthur went back upstairs, showered, tidied his bed up a bit and got his Maths book so he could look over some problems in the car on the way to school.

"I've put your lunch in your bag", said his Mum.

"Hurry up – we can't be late today!"

Arthur and Joseph got into the back of the car and put on their seat belts.

"Do you want me to test you again?" asked Joseph. He was a year younger than Arthur but he was a real brain box. Miss Jones had said that he was already a Level 3, which was quite exceptional for a Year 1 child. This had made his Mum feel proud and Arthur feel even more nervous about the exam.

"Okay", he said nervously and he handed the book over to Joseph. By the time they arrived at school, Arthur felt quite panic stricken. He could feel his heart beating faster and faster – almost as if it had popped up into his brain and was beating from inside his head.

"9 x 9 is 81, 9 x 9 is 81", he kept repeating to himself…. "Take one off … two up, multiply the 2 sides and it's cm^2…. cm^2! … 100cm is 1 metre and… yes, the 24 hour clock … it's 8.53 am that's 6 to 9 no 5 to 9 … no … it's …"

He stopped when he saw Mrs Maxwell ushering them into line ready to go straight into the classroom where the desks had all been set out in straight rows. He turned and looked towards his Mum. She was looking out of the car window and she gave him the thumbs up sign and mouthed "Good Luck".

Arthur just looked at her. He almost felt as if his feet were stuck in golden syrup and he couldn't pull them off the ground.

"I wonder if I shut my eyes and imagine it – then it will come true and I'll just sink into the ground and be stuck forever in a big pool of treacle – or better still…dark thick chocolate with nuts and raisins."

"Take your seats please, children", said Mrs Maxwell. She had two pink spots on her face – one on each cheek. Her voice sounded odd to Arthur – almost like she was just about to cry. Arthur sat down next to Marcos but they didn't talk to each other. He looked out of the window and then back towards Mrs Maxwell. He could just about hear what she was saying but he only got a few lines like "I can't stand it". "We ought to have at least 20 Level 3s this year…. Not with this lot … It's not fair on them or me…. Far too much stress for their age".

The test papers were placed on the tables and Mrs Maxwell told them all to turn them over and begin the test. Arthur felt as if his head was about to explode. He couldn't see what was on the test paper – it was like all the words and numbers had become blurred.

"I can't do it … I just can't", he said to himself. He turned round to look at everyone else. They all seemed to be writing away as if they had mega brains and could answer any question in the whole wide world.

Just then, he caught Marcos' eye. Marcos was taking a deep breath and then blowing it out into the air. He did this about six times and signalled to Arthur to do the same. Then Arthur remembered what Mrs Maxwell had taught them to do before, during and even after the tests in order to keep calm. He took a deep breath and let it out very slowly counting to 20 in his head. He did this three more times until his heart beat felt as if it was back in his heart and not in his head. Then he looked down at the paper. He read the first question… 10 + 4 … " That's okay", he thought, "I can do it …. It's not that hard". He looked down the first page and realised that he could actually do most of them. "Even if I can't get it, I'll just have a go anyway", he thought.

His hand still shook as he began to write down the first answer… but at least he'd finally started. That was the biggest hurdle, and he'd made it!

Discussion Time

The teacher can explain to the children that Arthur was experiencing stress in this story and can highlight some of his physical and emotional symptoms prior to focusing upon the following questions for discussion:

- What do they think 'stress' is?
- Who gets stressed? How and when?
- What happens when people get stressed? How do they respond?
- Can they identify something that has made them feel stressed like Arthur did? What did they do? How did they cope? Did they withdraw? Lose sleep? Cry or Shout?

Worksheet

The worksheet reinforces the variety of ways in which people respond to stress in their lives, and specifically the distinction between 'noisy' and 'quiet' responses. Children can work together in pairs or independently on this activity. Responses may include some of the following:

Noisy responses

- Shouting.
- Hitting out
- Arguing
- Destroying my work
- Picking a fight
- Hurting myself
- Hurting my friends and family.

Quiet responses

- Going to my room
- Crying quietly on my arm
- Not sleeping
- Not playing with my friends
- Hiding
- Pretend I don't hear
- Block things out.

Discussion

It may be useful to consider if there is any distinction between how boys and girls respond to stress. Are the boys noisy and the girls quiet? Is there such a distinction, or is this simply a stereotype?

Stress Stopper

The teacher can now introduce the first stress management strategy of a 'Stress Stopper', explaining to the children that even when we do feel stressed we can help ourselves to cope better if we use specific self-help strategies. Arthur provides an example of deep breathing and slow release of the breath whilst counting. In the story, the children can practise this strategy and identify specific stressful situations when this may be helpful to them. Personal targets may also then be set for the coming week. For example, "when I see a word I can't read and I get stressed, I'll take a deep breath and then count to 20 while I let my breath out slowly".

Follow up Work

- Design posters to illustrate the 'Stress Stopper'
- Complete a survey entitled 'What makes people feel stressed?'
- Investigate if there is a distinction between the responses to stress of boys and girls in the class by designing and completing simple 'Stress Questionnaires'
- Collect pictures of people who appear to be feeling stressed from newspapers, magazines and comics etc. and discuss how they may show such feelings and the causes of their anxieties and stress
- Discuss with the pupils if they have ever used the 'Stress Stopper'.

How People Respond to Stress

Sometimes they make a noisy response.
Record some of these in the box:

Sometimes they make a quiet response.
Record some of these in the box:

Session 2

Who gets affected
by stress?

Problem Parents for Paula

Paula felt herself dragging her feet along the pavement. She really didn't want to go home. School had ended over half an hour ago and it was really only a 10 minute walk to her block of flats – but she was dragging it out for all it was worth.

"Why are you walking so slowly Paula?" asked her best friend Kate. "Come on, move it along a bit. I've got a swimming lesson to get to before tea – and you're going to make me late if you dawdle like that."

"I'm sorry", said Paula... "It's just... I... I..." Kate could see that Paula was near to tears. She put her arm round her friend's shoulders and gave her a hug. "I'm sorry", she said. "I forgot ... are they still arguing?"

"Yep", said Paula. "It went on for hours and hours last night. They just keep screaming at each other."

"Never mind ... I'm sure it will be okay soon. Grown ups argue a lot, but they do sort it out", said Kate.

"I know, but I don't like it. It makes me feel like I've got butterflies in my stomach – I keep thinking that they'll argue so much that in the end, they'll just split up. I don't want my Mum and Dad to split up like Jason's did," said Paula.

"No – that would be horrible – but anyway, I'm sure they won't. I bet they'll have it sorted out by tonight. You'll see. Anyway, I've got to run – sorry Paula – or else I really will be late, see you later!" said Kate.

"See you later", said Paula.

She stopped to look at some flowers in Mrs Jones' garden. She felt so fed up and so worried, but also a bit angry too.

"It's not fair – why can't they just stop!" she thought to herself as she began to pick the heads off the rose bushes and then squash them into the ground.

She carried on walking very slowly and took out a piece of chalk from her bag. She held it up against Mr and Mrs Wright's wall and began to scribble along the side of it. Then she stopped and drew a big, angry monster face with its tongue poking out. She wrote 'Stop it!' underneath the face in a big speech bubble.

"I'm not going home yet", she thought. So she took herself off to the park and sat down on a swing. She swung herself higher and higher, almost hitting the bar at the top. Then she sat down on the bench and took out her packed lunch box. There was half an apple and one chocolate digestive left, so she ate both of these and then read her book. It was quite a good book – all about a boy who bullies people and then loses all his friends until he realises that he is very lonely and makes up with them all. She read the book all the way through and liked it so much that she decided to read it all again. By the time she'd read it three times she felt she almost knew it by heart. She looked around the park and suddenly realised that no one else was there.

"Oh no", she thought. "It must be past 6 o'clock when they lock the park up for the night – oh no! How will I get out – Mum will go mad!"

She ran up to the gates, and fortunately the park keeper was just locking up when she got there.

"Come on – hurry up", he said angrily. "Anyone would think you haven't got a home to go to." Paula felt like poking her tongue out at him and was just about to when she heard her Mum's voice behind her.

"Paula! Where have you been?" I've been worried sick about you!"

Then it was her Dad. "Not just worried", he said. "Extremely angry with you as well. We've had Mrs Jones on the phone saying that you picked all her roses and stamped on them and as if that's not enough, Mr Wright came banging on our door saying you'd been doing graffiti on the wall. Your mother and I are stressed out already and then you've you start behaving like I don't know what…. Well, what have you got to say for yourself?"

Paula looked down at her feet. She couldn't say anything. Then she began to cry – not a noisy crying – just the big, quiet tears that come when you feel like you've really had enough.

"Look", said her Mum, "We know you've been acting funny lately – you haven't been yourself – but we just can't have you upsetting the neighbours like that."

"Or staying out until it gets dark", said her Dad. He gave her his hand to hold and she took it because she knew it was his way of saying sorry for shouting. He'd been doing a lot of that recently and she didn't really feel that she could cope with hearing much more.

By this time, they'd got home and her Mum made a cup of tea.

"I think you need to explain", she said to Paula. Paula took a deep breath. "It's just that you two have been arguing so much and shouting at each other all the time. It… it made me feel bad, like I felt nervous and didn't want to come home. I thought you might be splitting up and I couldn't bear that." She gulped but managed to hold back her tears.

Her Dad was red in the face. Then he said, "Look, I think it's me that ought to explain. You see, there's been a lot of talk over at work and they're taking away my job and giving me another one, only it's not as much money."

"So you see, we've been stressed about the money", said her Mum and I've made it worse because I've been refusing to cancel our holiday because I think we need to get away. But your Dad says we can't afford it anymore and that he'd be more stressed than ever if we spent so much money on just two weeks away. But I've been having a hard time at work too so I decided that we needed the holiday. I've been insisting on it so that's why we've been arguing."

"Do you understand Paula?" asked her Dad.

"I think so – so, you're not going to split up?"

"No, of course not", said her Dad looking upset. "We love each other and you – that's the last thing we'd do."

Paula looked relieved.

"I think we just haven't been handling our stress very well", said her Mum "and neither have you".

"But I didn't know what to do", said Paula.

"Well, I think we all ought to talk about it a bit more and maybe we can sort things out before they get out of hand."

"Then you won't argue so much", said Paula half smiling.

"Now, now. Don't get cheeky", said her Mum. "Anyway, what can you suggest that will stop us arguing then?" she asked.

Paula thought hard.

"Well maybe we could just go to the seaside for one week instead of two. That way we would still get a holiday and you'd be resting from work and all the housework and it will be half the price, won't it? So you won't have to worry so much about the money Dad, will you?"

"No. I don't suppose he will", said her Mum, laughing.

"I'll drink to that", said her Dad, holding up his teacup. "Cheers".

Discussion Time

The teacher can explain to the children that everybody gets affected by stress at some point during their lives, which means that everyone should really try to work out ways of coping so that the stress does not cause them to permanently damage themselves or those around them. Children can then focus upon the following questions:

- How do parents get affected by stress?
- How do teachers get affected by stress?
- How do friends get affected by stress?
- How do brothers/sisters get affected by stress?
- What are the main causes of their stress? (e.g. time, money, work, peer pressure, media, tests, changes, relationships etc.)
- How do these people tend to react when they are stressed?
- How might they be able to help themselves more? (Refer to the story and the fact that Paula and her parents were able to find a solution once they actually sat down and talked things through together, i.e. adopted a joint problem solving approach).

Worksheet

The worksheet requires the children to identify the 'best way' to respond to others who are experiencing stress and who are reacting to it in a variety of ways. Children are asked to complete four statements as follows:

1. When somebody gets noisy the best way to respond is …
2. When somebody cries the best way to respond is…
3. When somebody gets aggressive the best way to respond is …
4. When somebody withdraws the best way to respond is…

Discussion

It may be helpful to 'brainstorm' these statements prior to asking the children to complete the activity sheet in order to reinforce the most helpful responses to each situation, and to highlight those responses that may not produce the best results, e.g. dragging someone who has withdrawn off to a party, shouting back at someone who is angry, stressed and very loud etc.

Stress Stopper

Paula goes to the park and begins to swing quite aggressively in order to 'get out' some of her anger and stress. Taking exercise is a good 'Stress Stopper'.

Moving around, jumping on the spot, shaking yourself up and down from your hands to your feet, and running around the playground, can all help to reduce stress levels and get rid of unwanted tensions. The children can identify their own forms of exercise and practise:

- running on the spot
- skipping on the spot
- 'shaking down' from head to toes.

Do all of these exercises with the pupils. Discuss with them what happens when we exercise. Do they know of any other physical ways of coping with stress?

Follow up Work

- Make a list of 'stress busting exercises'

- Have a three minute exercise session after lunch everyday for one week, and ask the children if they feel this has an impact upon:

  (a)   concentration
  (b)   stress levels.

- Design posters entitled 'Healthy Responses to Stress' and include exercise

- Discuss adults' and children's unhealthy responses to stress e.g. smoking, fighting, withdrawing, drinking too much, overeating etc.

- Discuss with pupils if they have ever used any of the 'Stress Stoppers'.

How People Respond to Stress

When somebody gets noisy,
the best way to respond is:

When somebody cries,
the best way to respond is:

When somebody gets
aggressive, the best way
to respond is:

When somebody withdraws,
the best way to respond is:

Session 3

The stress faced by young people

Barney's Bullies

Barney was looking forward to going to his new school, ever since he'd visited it during the summer term. They had all travelled down from Scotland for the half term week so that his Mum and Dad could look for a new house and so that they could also find him a school. His Dad had been transferred to London in May and since then he'd been living in a rented bed-sit until the end of the summer term when Barney and his Mum could join him. Barney knew that his Dad was really relieved that they were finally joining him.

"You'll never know how stressful the whole situation has been", he'd said to Barney's Mum on the telephone. Barney had been secretly listening in on the other telephone as he missed his Dad so much that he just wanted to hear his voice at every available opportunity – even though he knew this wasn't a good thing to do. Barney's Dad had explained how hard it was starting a new job without his family around him, living in one room and having to share a bathroom with six other men. Apparently, mornings were a nightmare so he'd eventually given up and started taking his showers last thing at night before he went to bed. Anyway it looked as though they'd all be much happier now. They'd found a 'nice house' in a 'good area' (according to his Mum). It was much smaller than their house in Scotland because the prices were just too expensive but it was near to Barney's new school – in fact, only a seven minute walk away. "Couldn't be easier", said Barney's Dad, squeezing his hand and giving him a wink. "Means we'll have even more time for those computer games when you get home from school."

Barney loved computers. He was a whizz on them and the best in his last school – not just in his year group, but in the whole school. "Not bad for a seven year old", his Mum had said proudly when she read his end of term report, which really only criticised him for not being good at P.E. Barney wasn't worried about that as he hated football anyway. He'd rather play on his computer that do anything else. But today, for once, he was more excited about something else. The thought of his new school was at the front of his mind. He just knew that he'd like it because it had the biggest computer suite and the most up to date equipment he'd seen in any school anywhere!

He smiled broadly as his Mum dropped him off at the gate. "Have a good time", she said. "I'll come and pick you up at 3.30 – bye". She walked off back to the house in order to get ready for her own first day in her new job. Fortunately, the builders' merchants round the corner had needed an accountant and it suited her down to the ground. She smiled – things seemed to be really good for all of them she thought to herself as she got home. Unfortunately, this wasn't to last – at least, not for Barney.

The day started fine. As he walked into the playground, he recognised two boys from his last visit who he knew would be in his Year 3 class. He walked towards them. "Hello", he said. I don't know if you remember – but I'm Barney – I saw you in June."

"Hi, yep, I do, I'm Jason", said one boy.

"And I am Sean", said the other. "I do remember you because you're from Scotland".

"That's right", said Barney.

"Yeah – they speak funny up there – like Och and Toch and all that", said Jason.

"Can you play football? Want a game? Who do you support?" said Sean.

"Nobody, I don't like football", said Barney. He could see the look of amazement in the faces of the two boys, but he'd always been told not to lie and to say what he was thinking so there was no backing down from it now.

"You mean you don't support anyone?"

"You don't play?"

"You don't even like it? You must be mad. Come on Sean – Let's leave the weirdo. Have you got your ball?"

The two boys ran off laughing. Barney looked away. He felt like an idiot. "I wish I could be like them but I'm just not", he thought to himself. "I can't make myself like it – it's just not fair – why can't they just accept it?"

But unfortunately, they couldn't. Just as he was considering this problem, Sean and Jason were talking to three other boys at the other end of the playground. They were laughing and pointing at him. After a few minutes one of the other boys shouted "Hey! Scottie! Carrot Head!" Another said, " Hey – you! The idiot who can't play football – what games do you play?"

Barney took a deep breath. He could feel his heart beating faster and he knew his cheeks were red as they felt really hot.

"I don't play games... I... I... play the computer."

"Oh no! He's a total nerd."

"It's nerdie Scottie – nerdie Scottie! nerdie Scottie!" They all began to shout. Barney felt as if he would explode. He was boiling hot and felt like charging at them until he saw that they were coming towards him. "I think he wants a fight", said one boy. Barney knew in an instant that it was the last thing he wanted. He wouldn't stand a chance with five boys against one. He didn't stop to think. He just ran. He ran as fast as he could, out of the school gates and down the road. He probably managed to get home in one minute flat. His Mum was just shutting the door on her way out.

"Oh no! Barney! What is it?" she said looking really concerned.

Barney couldn't speak for a moment – he was so out of breath. He stood on the spot and looked at his Mum panting loudly.

"Hold on", she said. "Just take a deep breath, calm down and tell me what's happened."

Barney didn't try to speak, he stopped for a minute to breathe slowly, then he explained everything to his Mum. She then took him back to school where they were immediately seen by the Headteacher who spent the next 25 minutes apologising for the behaviour of the boys concerned. She then assured Barney's Mum that the bullying would not happen again.

When Barney went into class, the five boys looked very embarrassed. Jason came up to him straight away and said "Look, I'm really sorry – we didn't mean to be so horrible –

we were just teasing at first and it got nasty. We didn't realise how upset it made you feel. So – anyway, I am sorry. You can sit with me if you want. We've got an I.T. lesson next. "Okay", said Barney, feeling relieved that Jason had apologised and also that his first lesson would be something he could do.

"I'm rubbish at I.T.", said Jason. "It's my worst thing. We can't afford a computer at home so everyone else is miles ahead of me."

"I'll help you", said Barney. "It's my hobby."

"What? Like football is mine?" asked Jason.

"Yeah – exactly", said Barney.

"Well – you help me and I'll teach you to be a referee – at least then you won't get left out of matches – even if you don't like playing the game."

Barney smiled. Things were looking up – just like his Mum had said.

Discussion Time

During this session it will be helpful to focus upon the psychological aspects of stress. The teacher can explain to the children how stress and associated feelings of anxiety and fear all have evolutionary significance and can help the process of human survival. The two main reactions to stress are 'fight' or 'flight' and in the story Barney chose the latter option – possibly because he could see that he was outnumbered. Similarly, cavemen who were confronted by fierce animals could also opt to stay and fight or simply run away in order to ensure their survival. It is important to highlight how we have similar reactions to stress – even if our stressors are not fierce animals. When stressed, all humans produce a chemical called adrenaline which heightens the senses, making the heart beat faster and preparing the body for a reaction. Children can focus upon the following questions:

- What makes us feel:

    (a)   Stressed?
    (b)   Frightened?
    (c)   Anxious?
    (d)   Angry?

- What reactions do we feel in our bodies? (e.g. heart beating faster, hair standing on end)
- When is stress useful to us? (e.g. we may try harder in a test or be more careful when crossing a busy road)
- When is stress less useful to us?

Worksheet

This worksheet reinforces the distinction between the pupils' positive and negative reactions to stress. It will be important to emphasise how maintaining a positive outlook and attempting to see the positive in every situation can also reduce stress and make it more manageable. This is an opportunity to reinforce the stress management skills learnt to date, and for children to identify their own personal strategies.

Discussion

It is a good idea to allow some time for children to feedback and share their ideas once they've completed the worksheet. This will enable the teacher to reinforce the distinction between negative and positive responses to stress, and to highlight the best and most useful strategies.

Stress Stopper

Visualising positives and learning to 'stop' and 'relax' are key strategies that need to be introduced to the children. It can be useful to select a piece of calming music to sit and listen to when you are feeling stressed, and to shut your eyes and try to create a positive image in your mind that is clearly associated with the music. The teacher can provide a short piece for the children to listen to and attempt this activity. It would be helpful to allow children to talk about how the music made them feel and what positive thoughts that it created for them.

Follow up work

- Create before, during and after pictures that show how human beings feel and respond at each stage in the stress situation
- Make use of children's literature on the topic of bullying in order to reinforce coping strategies and the importance of enlisting appropriate support. Useful books include:

  Willy the Wimp by Anthony Brown (Walker 1995)

  Bully by David Hughes (Walker 1995)

  The Trouble with the Tucker Twins by Rose Impey and Maureen Galvani (Puffin 1993)

  Rosie and the Pavement Bear by Susie Jenkin-Pearce (Red Fox 1992)

  The True Story of the Three Little Pigs by John Sciezka (Penguin 1991).

- Children can identify their own piece of 'peaceful music' to de-stress to. They can write a short description of how and why the music makes them feel calmer and less stressed.
- Discuss whether the pupils have ever used any of the 'Stress Stoppers'.

Session 3 Worksheet

How I React to Stress

Write or draw your ideas in the boxes

The good ways
I respond to stress

The negative ways
I respond to stress

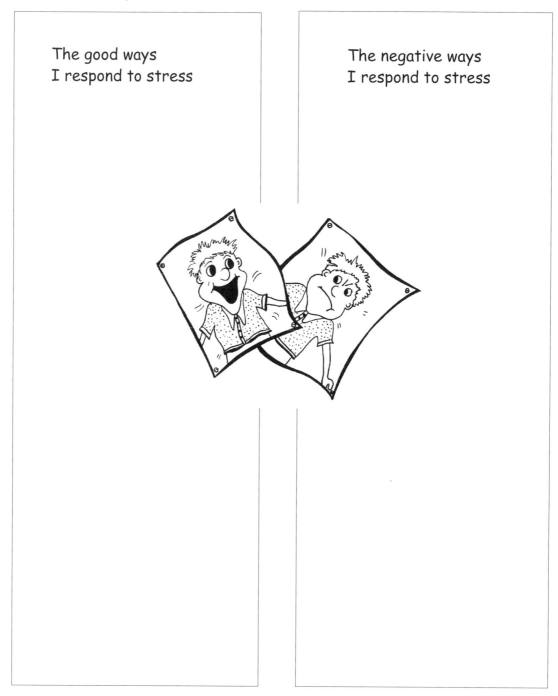

Session 4

Good ways to react
to stress

Worries for Wilma

Wilma was worried. She was worried yesterday, the day before that and for as long as she could remember. In fact, she had been worried before she came into her current Year 4 class and everyday since that first Monday in September. That was a lot of days, considering that it was now December and nearly Christmas. What was worse was that she knew why she was worried but she still hadn't got it sorted out. She'd done nothing to try to stop herself from feeling so bad. She hadn't told anyone – her friends, her Mum and certainly not her teacher, Mr Betts. That probably gives you a good idea about where her worries were coming from. Let me explain....

On the first day in her new class, Wilma had felt quite happy and excited as Mr Betts was a popular teacher. He had a big loud voice and big loud laugh and the children liked him a lot because he told funny stories and always gave gold stars – everyday of the week and not just on Fridays like the other teachers. She was looking forward to being in his class. The only thing she was worried about was whether she'd be able to understand the work. Other children had said that Year 4 work was much, much harder than Year 3 work. Not being the star pupil in the class (she found writing very hard), Wilma was already worried that she wouldn't be able to keep up. However, even at this stage, she didn't tell anyone about it because deep down she felt a bit ashamed at not being one of the clever ones. For them the work was always easy and they seemed to be able to do it all really quickly without making any mistakes. Wilma just couldn't work like that. She seemed to take far longer to get the hang of what the teacher wanted her to do and then, especially when she had to write things down, she seemed to take far longer than anyone else in the class to actually get the writing onto the page. She didn't know why. It just felt hard. She often couldn't remember how to spell words, so she'd have to look them up in her word book or try and sound them out in her head. That took longer and it made her feel upset and stupid when other people could write a word like 'special' in three seconds while it took her eight minutes to sort out the order of the letters. It just didn't seem, fair and it made her feel worried – very worried.

On the first day in hr new class all the children were asked to write a short piece entitled '10 things about me'. They had to write ten sentences and make sure that they used capital letters and full stops in the right places, and that they spelt the words correctly. That's what Mr Betts had said. Wilma could feel her heart beating faster. She already felt quite panic-stricken at the prospect of doing 10 whole sentences. She watched as Ben, Jo and Ella all started to scribble away. She sighed and picked up her pencil but she found it difficult to hold the pencil properly as her hand was shaking. She gripped the pencil in an attempt to stop the shaking but that only made her whole hand and wrist ache. She wrote 'My name is Wilma', by which time most of the other children at her table had finished. Mr Betts came over to their table to look at their work. He said "Well done" to the other children and pointed out a couple of spelling mistakes. He then turned to Wilma and said "Well, I must say that I'm glad you know your name is Wilma – that's at least one good thing!" He laughed loudly but Wilma didn't feel like laughing. She didn't see the joke. He then said, "You'll have to quicken up a bit now Wilma – remember – this is Year 4 now!"

It was that remark that sealed it. From then on Wilma was worried. She was worried everyday about her work and not being able to get it done quickly enough. So, she started to do the one thing that she knew she shouldn't do – she started copying other people's work. She knew that it was wrong and she knew that it wouldn't help her to learn her spellings or improve her writing – but she just couldn't help it. She felt so worried and this seemed to be the only way out. In, fact as far as she was concerned, it was the only way out and it worked – as long as she was careful and a bit clever about it. She would never copy a whole piece of work or even a whole sentence as she knew that Mr Betts would be able to see what she was doing straight away if she did that. What she did was to copy most of a sentence from someone else's piece of work and change one or two words. Then she'd copy the next bit from someone else's piece of work. She was always careful to make sure that it all made sense, but that was quite easy because they all tended to be writing about the same thing.

For example, if they were writing a poem entitled 'Autumn Leaves' she could easily copy a sentence from Ella, 'Autumn leaves fall to the ground' and another sentence from Jo 'Gold, red, yellow, orange and deep brown' and finally from Ben 'Gently floating down, down, down' and so on. Although her heart beat loudly throughout this process, she was able to write at twice the speed as she didn't have to stop all the time in order to look up her spellings.

So she had managed this very well for quite some time – until today. Today was different because Mr Betts had asked them all to do a timed piece of independent writing under what he called 'test conditions'. This meant that they all had to sit on separate desks, facing the front and not talking to anyone – just like they'd done in their SAT tests in Year 2. Wilma was more than worried. She felt sick with panic and fear. She just knew that she couldn't do it. She felt hot and put her hand to her throat. She could feel her pulse beating like a big bass drum in her neck. She felt her stomach twist and knot up.

"I'm going to be sick", she thought and almost without thinking, she stood up and ran outside to the girls toilets. She bent over the sink nearest to the door and was sick – very, very sick. The tears were streaming down her face and she felt as though she was choking. Mrs West the Welfare Assistant came in behind her and put her arm round her shoulder.

"That's it Wilma – just get it all out", she said. She wiped her forehead and around her mouth with a damp cloth. "Do you think that's it?" she asked. Wilma nodded and then she started to cry.

Mrs West said, "There, there – what is it? You don't need to cry Wilma", and she gave her a cuddle, which of course made Wilma cry even more.

Eventually she stopped and turned to say sorry to Mrs West but Mrs West would have none of it. "You certainly shouldn't apologise for being sick Wilma – that's no-one's fault. You must have eaten something that had gone off a bit."

"No, I... I didn't", stuttered Wilma.

"Well – there must have been something", said Mrs West.

"There is.... A... a ... and.... It is all my fault", whimpered Wilma. "You see. .. I've ... b...been cheating for so long and I was going to get found out and that's why I was s...s...sick because I got so worried about b...b...being f...f...found out." She took a deep breath. "I think you should tell me all about it", said Mrs West. "You know.... we can nearly always get things sorted out if we talk about it. You know what they say - a problem shared is a problem halved."

And of course, Mrs West was right. Once Wilma had explained everything and told her all about how hard she found the writing and spelling everything, just took a turn for the better. Mrs Bhattercherjee gave her extra special lessons for English, and Mr Betts gave her work that she could really do in lessons so that she didn't need to feel so dumb anymore, and most importantly she didn't need to cheat or get worried. In fact, she made such a big improvement over the Spring Term that Mr Betts gave her a new nickname of Wilma Wizard and every time she did more than four sentences in 10 minutes he wrote 'Wizard piece of work' on her writing and gave her two gold stars. How much better it was to be called 'Wizard Wilma' rather than being 'Worried Wilma!'

Discussion Time

It is important to point out that we cannot magically make all our stressors disappear. There are some that we will simply have to learn how to manage. In the story, Wilma feels stressed by her poor literacy skills and subsequently uses negative strategies to try and hide them from her teacher and peers. She may well not be able to develop her literacy skills to the same level as those of her brightest peers, which means she will have to live with the fact that she may always need to work a bit harder for less of a result. This is a stressor that she will have to manage and cope with. Lying and covering up are not useful strategies, but working hard, being honest and asking for and receiving the kind of help and support she needs certainly are.

Children can focus on the following questions:

- How do we react 'badly' to stress? (e.g. not sleeping, withdrawing, saying nasty things etc.)
- What are 'good' reactions to stress?
- Who can help us to develop good reactions?
- How can we help each other to cope with stress more effectively?

Worksheet

The worksheet reinforces each child's positive skills and strategies in terms of coping effectively with stress. Children are asked to identify four strategies that they use and these need to be presented as 'good' ways to respond to stress. This is also a further opportunity to reinforce the stress management strategies covered to date for example:

- Deep breathing
- Counting to 20 and letting your breath out slowly
- Jumping on the spot
- Running out the stress
- Listening to 'calm' music
- Skipping
- 'Shaking down' from head to toe etc.

Discussion

What strategies can be used and what strategies have they tried?

Stress Stopper

In the story, Wilma is able to sort out her problem and relieve her stress by talking it through with Mrs West. A solution directly results from their conversation and Mrs West's view that a 'problem shared is a problem halved!'

Children need to know that friends and adults can support them. Working together and talking through a problem in order to find the best possible solution is a key 'Stress Stopper' that can be learnt and practised.

Children can identify a range of 'typical' problems that they may face, both in and out of school. These can be written down onto a small card and children can then work together in pairs in order to 'talk through to a solution'. It will be beneficial to also allow some time for feedback from each pair and to highlight the best and most appropriate strategies and solutions to each problem.

Follow up Work

- Children can make 'Stress Stopper' booklets, recording all the strategies and methods that they have learnt and practised to date
- Reinforce the importance of talking to friends, teachers and parents about worries and problems by reading *Sam's Worries* by Maryann MacDonald and Judith Riches (ABC, 1995). In this story, Sam is worried about absolutely everything. His Mother tries to reassure him, but it is talking to his teddy bear that really helps in the end
- Children can write stories entitled 'A problem shared is a problem halved'
- Discuss fears and phobias and how these can be overcome by children and adults alike
- Discuss with the pupils if they have used any of the 'Stress Stoppers'.

Developing your Skills to Cope with Stress

1) I could…

2) I could…

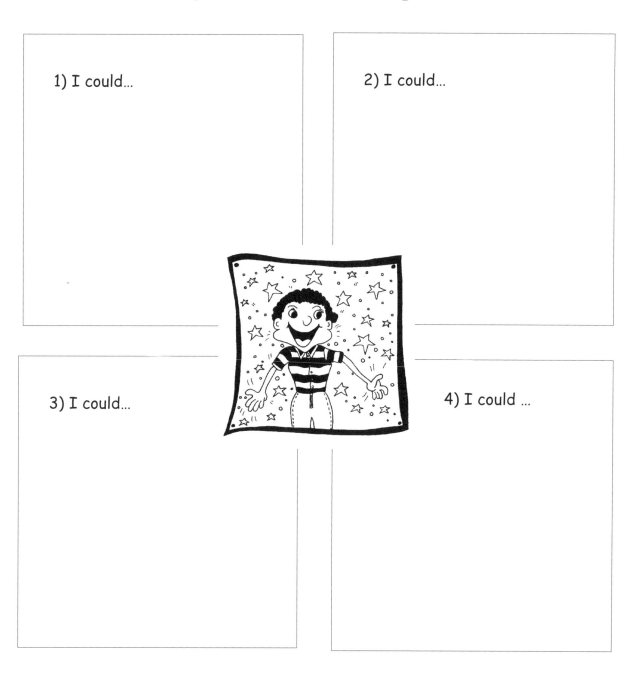

3) I could…

4) I could …

Session 5

New ways of coping

with stress

Fred's Friends

Fred had been friends with Ben and Shazia since he first came to Northfield Primary School. In fact, they had all been at the Nursery together and then gone through each of the subsequent classes right up until Year 3 where they were now. They'd had ups and downs like most friends do, but they all liked to do the same kinds of things and generally got on very well. This was true both in and out of school. Every Wednesday after school they all went to the Gymnastics Club and then they would take it in turns to go to each other's houses for tea. That was good fun – especially when their Mums let them have sleepovers and they could raid the fridge for a midnight feast. They even walked to school with each other now as they all lived in Murcott Avenue just six minutes from the Junior entrance and then of course, they all sat at the same table in Mr Pitman's class. Fred felt happy. He had good friends and he always had a lot of fun – at least, that is, until last week. That's when all the problems began.

That's when he noticed that his friends were acting very strangely – they were definitely different!

On Monday morning, Fred had called at Ben's house as he usually did before they both went to pick up Shazia. That was the first time that he felt that something was up. Ben's Mum came to the door and smiled at him just like she usually did. Fred was all ready to jump in and shout "Hurry up Ben!" like he usually did, when Ben's Mum said, "It's okay Fred! No need to give him the wake-up call today. He's already gone. He went off with George at 7.30 a.m. They've both joined the Swimming Club. They're going twice a week now – on Mondays and Wednesdays – so you won't need to call for him." She smiled and shut the door.

Fred felt something turn in the pit of his stomach. It wasn't a comfortable feeling. He couldn't understand why Ben hadn't told him anything about the swimming club and why he hadn't asked him to go as well? Why had he asked George? George wasn't even a special friend of theirs. He wasn't in their gang. Fred shook his head as if he thought it might help to sort out his confusion. No, he certainly didn't feel comfortable. He felt a bit confused and left out and if he was really honest, perhaps even a little jealous. He turned and walked up the road to Number 29 and knocked there. Shazia's Dad came to the door.

"Hello Fred", he said. "How are you?"

"Fine thanks", lied Fred. "Is Shazia ready?"

"Yes she's just coming – but you'll have to come in and wait for a moment as she's got her cousin here from India and she's going to be coming to school with you both as well. I think they're both a bit too excited about it actually. They seem to have spent the last hour and a half deciding what they're going to wear – so you'll just have to bear with them for a bit!"

Fred went in and sat down in front of the T.V. He could hear the two girls laughing and giggling together upstairs. They were chatting away without appearing to pause for breath. They obviously had a lot to say to each other and Fred wondered how he was going to manage to get a word in as well. Then Shazia came bursting through the door.

"Hello Fred – meet my cousin, Amrita. She's going to live with us now until she's eighteen so she's coming to school with us – she's going to be in our class and sit at our table. Isn't it brilliant!" She looked really happy and excited. Fred said how good it would be and said hello to Amrita but he found it hard to smile. All the way to school, the two girls chatted away excitedly and Shazia hardly spoke to Fred at all – in fact only to say, "You'll have to sit at the other end of the table Fred because Amrita needs to sit next to me so I can translate for her. Also, as she's new she should be next to the one she knows best and that's me." She gave her cousin a hug. Both girls giggled as they went into the classroom.

Then there was another surprise for him. Sitting next to Ben at their table and looking as pleased as anything with himself, was George. The two boys were so intent on discussing what they had to do in order to get their next swimming badge, that they didn't even notice Fred as he sat down at the other end of the table. He looked over towards the four children who all seemed to be so happy and who also all seemed to be ignoring him. "I don't get it", he thought to himself. "Why has it all changed so suddenly? Why am I being left out?"

Fred felt very tense. The knot inside his stomach seemed to be getting tighter and tighter. And of course, things only seemed to get worse. Throughout the literacy lesson Shazia had to translate everything for Amrita and George was continually asking Ben for help. Fred had to work on his own. He was beginning to get angry. "It's not fair", he thought. "Why am I not being included?"

It got worse at breaktime. Shazia didn't want to play football as she usually did because she wanted to show Amrita around the playground and play hopscotch. George and Ben didn't want to play either as they were both too interested in reading the swimming magazine that they'd picked up in the club that morning. Fred had felt left out earlier – but now he felt as if he was going to either explode or cry. When they got back into class he sat down in his chair with a thump and put his elbows onto the table in an effort to calm himself down. Just then, George turned round to him and said, "Fred do you think you can help me with this sum? Ben says that you're the best in the class at sums and I'm really rubbish at them. Can you explain it?"

Fred looked surprised – first of all that he was being spoken to by George at all – and then at himself as he heard himself say "Yeah – alright – which one is it?"

George explained and Fred talked him through the answer. Then Shazia turned and said "Amrita says that she'd like to learn to play football Fred, and she wants to know if you can teach her at lunchtime – just the basics you know. I think it's better that you do it because we'll only get the giggles if I try and she'll learn nothing then. What do you think?" Fred shrugged and said "Okay" almost without thinking, but he did stop and think later on that day. He thought how glad he was that he'd stopped himself from getting stressed out and angry and that he had agreed to help George and Amrita, because now he had four friends instead of two. Also, instead of being on his own and feeling left out, he was now about to try and fit two extra friends into two bunk beds for a mega sleepover. Isn't it funny how things can turn out if you make the right decision, which is of course just what Fred had done!

Discussion Time

The story touches on the kinds of stresses that result from change, and specifically changes in friendships, that children will frequently encounter both in and out of the school context. It is important to acknowledge how strong reactions to such changes can be and how we need to be able to stop, think and reflect before we respond to others and to the stressors in our lives.

Children can focus upon the following questions:

- What kinds of changes cause us to feel stressed?
- How can we cope better with these changes? (i.e. identifying who
  can help us and how we can help ourselves).

What is vital is that children understand that they can play a part in both a joint problem solving process (with friends/adults) and in using individual problem solving techniques. It will be helpful to introduce the Traffic Light Method (a stepped approach to sorting stress) at this point in the discussion and to highlight how this is a useful tool for solving a range of problems.

This method encourages the children to visualise traffic lights and make use of a series of reflection questions in order to develop the best solution. It would be helpful to identify a range of problems and write these up onto a white board/flip chart.

Children could then work individually, in pairs or in small groups in order to problem solve by using the Traffic Light Method. Use the Traffic Light worksheet and give the pupils specific scenarios to work on. Stress situations/problems might include some of the following:

- My best friend isn't talking to me
- No one wants to play with me
- My Mum and Dad keep arguing
- My brother keeps bullying me
- I'm scared of my teacher
- The sums are too hard
- I hate swimming as I'm scared of putting my head under the water
- The dark frightens me
- There's a test on Friday
- I don't like my Step Dad.

Worksheet

The worksheet introduces a relaxation strategy that children can use when they feel stressed. The activity is called 'A Peaceful Place' and children are asked to shut their eyes and imagine being in a peaceful place that will make them feel calm, happy and relaxed.

They are then required to draw/write about this place on the worksheet. It may also be helpful for children to identify a time during the week or during a specific day when they feel that they will be able to successfully make use of this visualisation strategy.

Discussion

Is the Traffic Light Method useful? Did anybody try the relaxation technique?

Stress Stopper

The teacher can introduce a Relaxation Script to the children and provide opportunities for them to use this whilst in school. It may be helpful to set out a circle of chairs and ensure that the room is quiet with no distractions. The children should all be seated in a chair with both their feet planted firmly on the ground and their legs uncrossed. The script could then be read out as follows, or devised entirely by the teacher:

1. Put your hands in your lap and close your eyes.
2. Wrinkle your forehead as if you are angry, then relax and feel your forehead become smooth.
3. Close your lips tightly, then let go and feel your mouth, face and neck relax all over.
4. Lift your shoulders up towards your ears, circle them round a couple of times, then let them drop and relax.
5. Clench your fists, then loosen your fingers and relax your hands and arms.
6. Pull in your tummy, hold it tightly then relax and breathe slowly and evenly. Feel your back sink into the chair.
7. Tense the muscles in your legs, then release them and relax.
8. Press your feet into the floor as hard as you can, then relax.
9. Curl up your toes tightly, then relax.
10. Finally, let yourself relax all over. Feel the tension drain away from your head, neck, shoulders, tummy, legs and toes. Imagine it flowing down and out of your body. Your feet feel heavy and relaxed, sinking into the floor. Heavier and heavier, more and more relaxed. Breathe in deeply, and slowly let your breath out, relaxing a bit more with each breath. Count down from 10 to 0 and then open your eyes.

Enjoy feeling relaxed and calm.

Follow up Work

- Focus on how changes can cause stress – particularly those involving relationships with friends and family and how we can cope with such changes if we make use of the stress management strategies that we have learnt in these lessons. Children's literature can act as a starting point for such discussions. For example: *Changes* by Anthony Browne (Walker) is a fascinating examination of both the inner and outer world of change by a master picture book artist. The protagonist, Joseph Kaye, has an amazing day when everything seems to change. His own fears of what change really means manifest themselves in a series of extraordinary illusions e.g. the kettle changing into the cat. Finally, he is back in the reality of his family life and what it's like to have a new baby sister. *Learning Mrs Ellis* by Catherine Robinson and Sue Broadley

(Bodley Head) tackles the stress of changing teachers and deals very well with the sense of loss that children experience. *Badger's Parting Gifts* by Susan Varley (Julia MacRae) is an extremely useful story for dealing with any kind of loss or change in a child's life. The story details how, when Badger dies, all the other animals find it extremely difficult not to be sad. However, they soon begin to realise that each one of them has a very special memory of Badger - something that he'd taught them that they could do really well. This was his parting gift to them, something that they could always treasure.

- You could develop the idea of a Peaceful Place with more work on guided imagery (*Picture This* by Murray White [1999] Lucky Duck Publishing).

- Children can update their Personal 'Stress Stopper' Booklets (as detailed in Session 4) with the new stress management strategies introduced in this session.

- Children can focus upon the skills that make a good friend e.g. one who listens, keeps secrets, helps you with problems, makes you laugh etc. They can devise illustrated lists/ poems on this topic.

- Discuss with the pupils if they have ever used any of the 'Stress Stoppers'.

- Finally the teacher can award each child the certificate provided. This can be awarded in order to both congratulate each child for participating and to recognise and highlight the fact that they have learnt how to cope with stress and keep cool! You can turn this into a celebration. Ask some significant other in the school to present the certificates. Create a party atmosphere. Involve the pupils. Set them the problem, you want to have a party but you are too 'stressed' to organise it. Can they solve your problem and reduce your stress!

The Traffic Light Method
A Stepped Approach to Sorting Stress

Stop! ...and calm down

1) What is the problem?

Wait!

2) What is the feeling?

3) List some possible solutions

1

2

3

Go!   4) Make a plan

A Peaceful Place

Shut your eyes and imagine a peaceful place where you will feel calm, happy and relaxed. Draw or write about your peaceful place.

My Peaceful Place

This Certificate is Awarded to:

. . . .

Congratulations!

You have learnt how to cope with stress and keep your cool!

Signed   Date

. . . .

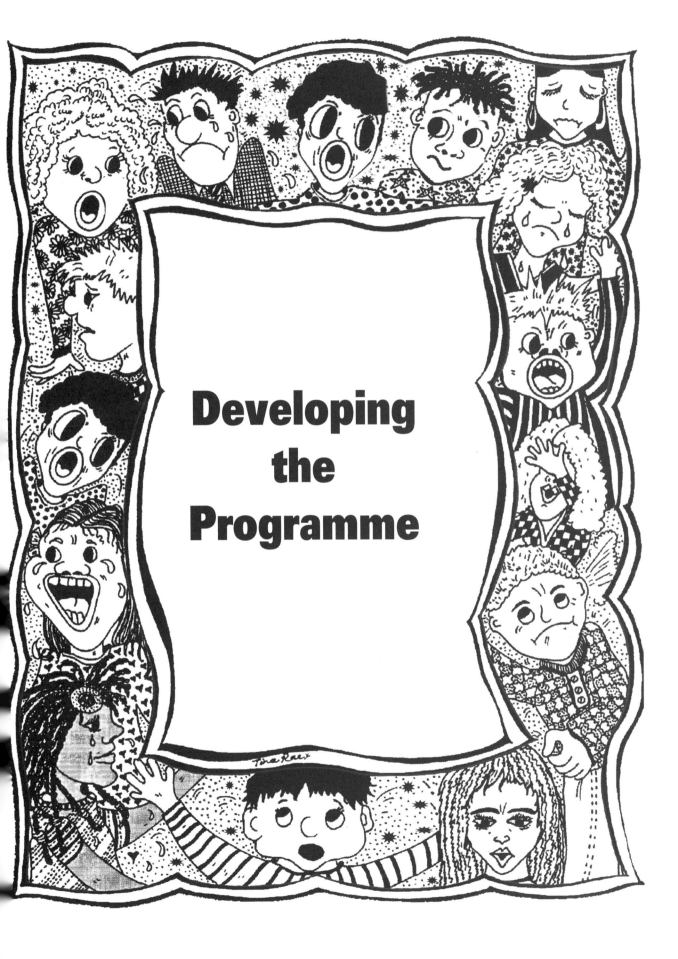

Developing
the
Programme

Developing the Programme

We hope you found this programme useful and that the objectives identified on page 7 have been achieved. We see this type of work as part of the way we can assist young people to develop their emotional intelligence.

Working with teachers in Bristol, the following core elements of an emotional curriculum were identified:

Self-awareness

- Observing yourself and recognising your feelings
- Building a vocabulary for feelings
- Knowing the relationship between thoughts, feelings and actions.

Managing Feelings

- Handling feelings so that they are appropriate
- Realising what is behind a feeling
- Finding ways to handle fears, anxiety, anger and sadness.

Empathy

- Understanding others' feelings and concerns
- Appreciating differences in how people feel about things.

Communication

- Talking about feelings effectively
- Becoming a good listener
- Sending 'I' messages instead of blame.

Problem-solving and Decision-making

- Examining your actions and knowing their consequences
- Knowing if thought or feeling is ruling a decision
- Making choices between options for action.

(For a fuller description of this work see *The Emotional Curriculum – A Developmental Progression'* in *The Emotional Literacy Hour* Gross *et al* 2000.)

Children learn in a variety of ways and you might like to consider the following:

The Adults in Schools as Good Role Models

Do the adults in your school provide good models for the pupils? Much of our learning is acquired from the models around us. Are you confident that all the adults demonstrate the skills of an emotionally literate person?

The Right Atmosphere

We have to provide the conditions that assist emotional development. Many mission statements in primary schools talk about developing young people who will have self-control and be self-motivated. However, the systems used to control behaviour do not seem to provide the conditions that allow this type of self-development.

You might wish to consider the core elements of an emotional curriculum. Does your school/ classroom provide a supportive environment to assist young people's emotional development? Circle Time is one way of providing an opportunity for young people to explore emotional issues in a safe way. Ballard (1982) describes Circle Time as a way of developing:

- awareness – knowing who I am
- mastery – knowing what I can do
- social interaction – knowing how I function in the world of others.

Bliss et al (1995) wrote: "Circle Time is an inter-related, interactive, multi-layered process. Within the Circle participants learn about self, learn about others, and relate this knowledge to build relationships between individuals and between groups. The aims for self are to:

- communicate needs
- understand the needs of others
- increase confidence, raise self-esteem." (p6)

Teaching the Skills Needed for Emotional Development

As well as providing good role models and a supportive environment, we also need to teach skills. This book provides the opportunity to help young people learn ways of managing stress. Consider the core elements of an emotional curriculum, are you directly teaching the skills required for an emotionally literate person? We acknowledge that schools identify and teach a variety of skills related to 'academic learning'. However, we note that 'emotional learning' is not so clearly taught. We expect young people to acquire emotional skills. Our challenge is that this is such an important part of learning, we should not leave it to chance. We should teach these skills if we want our young people to be able to:

- express feelings
- have a vocabulary of feelings
- be a good listener
- be a problem solver.

Useful Resources

Lucky Duck Publishing has grown since its first publication in 1988, and is now one of the UK's largest publishers of books on positive behaviour management. We have books and videos on a variety of topics including:

- Circle Time
- Mediation
- Bullying
- Self Esteem
- Anger Management
- Social Skills.

Visit our website (www.luckyduck.co.uk) for our current publication list. Alternatively, phone 0117 973 2881 or fax 0117 973 1707 for our catalogue.

Front Covers for Pupils' Worksheets

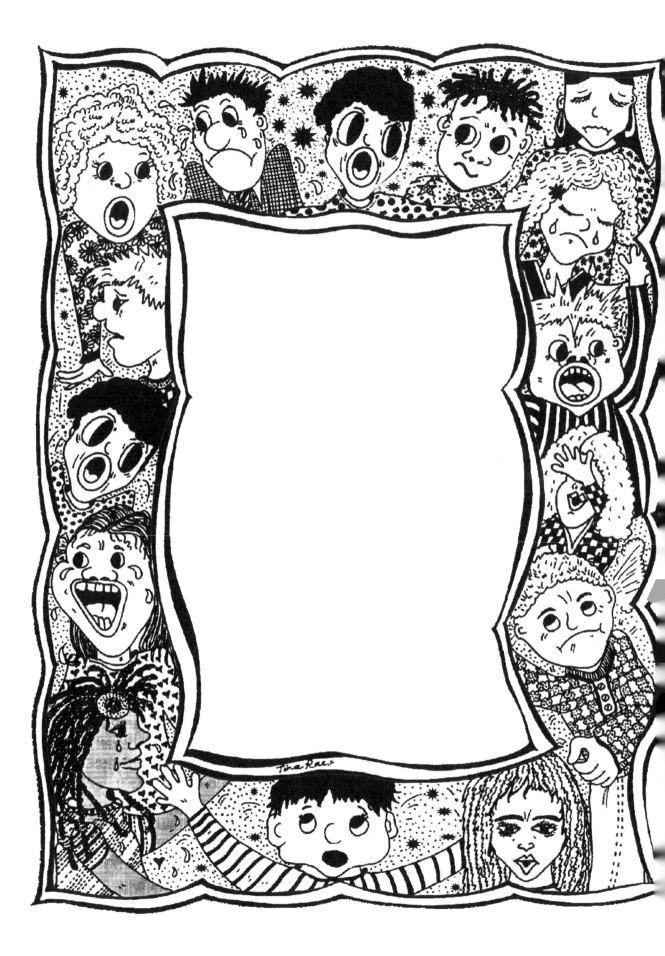